The Howling Stones

'The Howling Stones'
An original concept by Amanda Brandon
© Amanda Brandon 2022

Illustrated by Izzy Evans

Published by MAVERICK ARTS PUBLISHING LTD
Studio 11, City Business Centre, 6 Brighton Road,
Horsham, West Sussex, RH13 5BB
© Maverick Arts Publishing Limited February 2022
+44 (0)1403 256941

A CIP catalogue record for this book is available at the British Library.

ISBN 978-1-84886-867-0

www.maverickbooks.co.uk

This book is rated as: Grey Band (Guided Reading)

The Howling Stones

Written by
Amanda Brandon

Illustrated by
Izzy Evans

Chapter 1

The full moon glimmered in the inky black sky. *Swish, swish!* The trees whispered as the midnight hour approached.

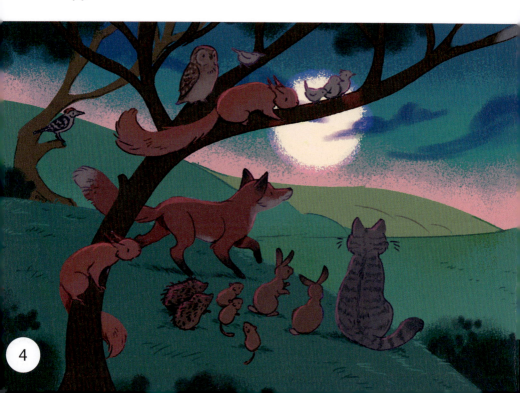

"AWOOo!"

The watching woodland animals tensed. Their eyes were fixed on the seven large rocks set in a circle in the clearing below them. Twigs snapped and an owl hooted a warning. In the darkness, a pack of wolves approached the sacred Howling Stones. Their silvery fur gleamed in the moonlight. They slowly padded one by one around the Stones. They had reached their meeting place. Tonight there was a special ceremony.

Seven wolves slipped from the pack and formed an inner circle. They were the Howling Stone Elders. All seven of them howled together. Their song echoed around the woodland.

Randall Wolf stepped out of the watching crowd into the centre of the circle.

The moon's beam highlighted his gleaming teeth. He lifted his head. His nose quivered and he let out his own loud howl in return.

Chief Wolf Quicksilver approached Randall. He was an older wolf with a patch of grey across one eye. "Welcome, Randall," Quicksilver said. "You have been given the role of being a woodland guardian."

Randall bowed his head, and Quicksilver tapped him on the head with his paw.

"Remember," Quicksilver said, "it is a great honour to look after our wonderful home. Use your skills wisely to protect it."

The woodland creatures held their breath. They watched the ceremony in awe from their hiding places in the trees surrounding the Stones. When Quicksilver stepped back, they clapped and cheered.

Randall puffed out his chest. "I won't let you down," he said.

The Elders nodded. They circled the Stones one last time before they disappeared into the wood. Randall followed. He held his head high. At last he was a woodland guardian—just like his father and grandfather before him.

The next day, the sun shone bright and Randall woke early. He was determined to start his new duties as quickly as possible. He had to make sure the wood was clear of human rubbish which might endanger the animals.

He grabbed a sack in his mouth and set off through the wood. "Tsk, tsk," he grumbled as he spied a pile of picnic litter. "People should take this home with them."

Soon his sack was full. He decided to take a rest by an old tree stump.

"Being a guardian is hard work." He yawned and his eyes drooped. The excitement of last night had begun to take its toll. He decided to have a nap.

His eyes had just closed when he heard a cry.

"Help! Help!"

Chapter 2

Randall raised his head. Where had that come from?

"Help! Help! I'm trapped!"

He turned and peered through the canopy of trees to the left of him. There it was again.

"Help! Help!"

His ears strained and a stir of excitement swirled in his stomach. "Someone's in trouble. Now I'm a guardian, it's my job to help."

He called out, "Hold on! Woodland guardian to the rescue."

Randall pushed his way through some bushes. On the other side was a pile of heavy logs. He stopped.

There was no one there.

Where had the cry come from?

"Over here, I'm stuck in the logs," a small voice cried.

Randall bounded over to the pile of freshly cut logs and peered between them.

"Down here. A log fell and now I can't squeeze back."

In the darkness of the log pile, Randall spied two bright eyes.

He walked around the logs. They were stacked high. "There are too many and they are too heavy to move on my own," Randall said. "They could crash down and squash us both." He shuddered.

Then he saw a small gap at the end of the pile.

"Can you wriggle to this end? Then I might be able to pull you through," he said to the creature hidden in the logs.

There was a scrabble and a squeal followed by silence. Randall wondered whether he'd done the right thing. Then a pink nose poked through the gap between the logs.

Randall peered in. He could now see it was a rabbit. "This may hurt a little but bend forward as far as you can," he said. "I'm going to pull."

Randall tugged. The logs moved a little and he gulped. He stumbled backwards as a brown rabbit with pink paws squeezed out and landed on his chest with a **THUD!**

"Phew! Thanks for that. I could have been trapped forever!" The rabbit held out a paw. "I'm Flo by the way."

"Randall, woodland guardian," he grinned and held out his furry paw in return. "It's all part of the service. It's my duty to protect the woodland and all its creatures."

"That sounds like a big task," Flo said. "I expect you've had to rescue lots of animals though, not just a silly bunny who was being nosy."

"Well, not exactly. It's my first day."

"Wow! Then I'm your first rescue. I feel honoured. You did a marvellous job." Flo gave him a big smile.

Randall felt his cheeks turn red. "It was nothing," he said but his chest puffed out and he couldn't help grinning again.

"Well I'd better be off then. Perhaps I'll see you on your next patrol," Flo gave a couple of small hops and turned towards the wood.

"Watch out for log piles," Randall joked.

But before Flo reached the trees, there was a rumbling sound. "Oh no! What's that?" She turned to Randall with a look of alarm.

"I don't know," he replied. "It's coming nearer. It sounds like the whirr of machinery."

Flo's anxious face looked up at him. She gulped and said, "Could it be... humans?"

Randall tried not to look worried but a shiver ran through him. He always hid when he heard that sound. Where could they hide? He pulled Flo back towards a large oak tree.

They pressed against the trunk and glanced around. The sound grew louder. Randall looked up. The branches of a large tree to the side of them swayed back and forth. The leaves swished high above them.

There was a loud crack and a roar.

"TIMBER!" a shout came from beyond the trees.

"That definitely sounds like humans," Randall said. Flo covered her ears with her paws as the cracking echoed all around them.

"Run!" she shouted.

Randall opened his jaw and grabbed Flo by the scruff of the neck, then pulled her in the opposite direction.

But it was too late. The tree crashed down towards them. Randall threw them both to one side, out of the way. They tumbled down a slope and landed in a mass of ferns.

Randall groaned. He rolled over to find Flo was gone.

Chapter 3

Randall gasped. He scrabbled amongst the leaves. "Flo! Flo! Where are you?" His heart raced and branches and twigs scratched his paws. He ignored the pain.

Suddenly two brown ears popped up to the right of him.

"What happened?" Flo rubbed her eyes and looked dazed.

"The tree crashed down and nearly flattened us."

"But that noise. What was it?" Flo wrinkled her nose and brushed her whiskers. Her gaze darted from side to side.

Randall gulped. "I'm guessing humans are cutting down trees. That's why there was that enormous log pile."

"Well I think we should get out of here. It's not safe."

"You're right. Come on! Let's go. I'll take you home."

Randall grabbed the litter sack and the two of them headed deeper into the wood.

They hadn't gone far when they heard a familiar whirring sound. "Oh no! Not again!" Flo cried in alarm. She hopped on Randall's back. "Hurry!"

Randall bounded forwards, but one of his front paws caught in a twisted tree stump hidden by leaves and he stumbled. Flo's paws clasped his neck tight as she clung on. Randall dropped his sack. The contents scattered free.

He tried to gather the litter into his sack again. "There's no time," Flo hurried him.

Randall reluctantly turned and raced on. It was hard to run with a rabbit clinging to him. When he reached Flo's home, he collapsed on the ground. Flo hopped off. His sack was empty. "I'll have to start all over again tomorrow," he said with a sigh.

"Hang on. What's this?"

A picture of some red-brick homes with cars and people fluttered loose from the sack. There was a map of the Howling Stones with a cross through it.

He gulped. A chill ran through him. "Look, Flo! That's why all the trees are being cut down. Humans want to build homes on our sacred site. What are we going to do?"

Chapter 4

That night, Randall joined the other wolves in their nightly ceremony at the Howling Stones. Flo waited until they'd finished.

"Why didn't you say anything about the Stones?" Flo said, her eyes wide with concern.

Randall frowned. "I know I'm a guardian and it's my job to protect everything in the wood. But hush! Don't tell anyone yet. It will only make them worry. I'm sure I can save the Stones by myself."

"Are you sure? Well, I suppose you saved me twice today. You are so brave. If anyone can do it, you can." Flo snuggled close to Randall. His warm fur tickled her nose.

Randall didn't feel very confident but he put a reassuring paw on her shoulder and ignored the heaviness in the pit of his stomach. He didn't want to let Flo or the Elders down. He frowned and thought hard.

"**AWOOO!**" He gave one final howl.

"Ooh, wolf howls always sound so spooky and mysterious." Flo gave a little shiver.

Randall gasped. "Thanks, Flo! You've just given me a brilliant idea."

"Me! What did I say?" Flo looked puzzled but Randall just grinned.

The next day, the two of them returned to the spot where the tree had crashed down. In the distance they saw two men with bright yellow hard hats. There was the familiar cry of "Timber!" and another tree was felled. But this time Flo and Randall hid well back.

"I'm going to scare the workers away. Three or four

blood-curdling howls should do the trick," he told Flo.

"Ooh do be careful." She hopped up and down.

Randall cleared his throat and let out an enormous,

" AWOOo!"

Nothing happened.

He waited until the noise of the machinery paused then he tried again. This time he let his howl come from the

bottom of his toes. It rose up through his belly and then, *boom!* It came rushing out.

But the workers carried on and another tree crashed down. The humans took no notice of Randall's cries.

When one of them stepped closer in their direction, Randall howled one of his biggest howls. "Ha! Gotcha!" he grinned afterwards.

But the worker turned away and carried on sawing the tree into logs. "What the...?" Randall spluttered.

"Look!" Flo pointed. "The workers are wearing huge ear defenders to drown out the noise of the machinery. That's why they can't hear your howls."

Randall sank to the ground. His throat was sore from howling. He sighed and said, "It looks like I'll have to come up with another plan."

Chapter 5

That night, Randall tossed and turned. He wondered how he could stop the humans. His first attempt had failed. What else could he do to protect the Howling Stones? He scratched his ears and thought hard. But, try as he might, he was all out of ideas.

When the sun came up, he had barely slept. He yawned and rolled over onto his litter sack. It was scratchy and uncomfortable. Randall grumbled. He grumbled throughout breakfast and he was still grumbling when he stepped out of his den. Flo arrived and he could barely manage to say, "Hi."

"Sorry, I'm just grumpy because I can't think of a plan," he added.

Flo didn't say anything. She just patted his paw and looked sad.

"Ah well," Randall rose and grabbed his sack. "I might as well do something useful today in the wood."

"I'll help you," Flo said, and she hopped alongside him as they made their way through the wood. "Looks like Haley Squirrel has tidied up her acorn pile." She picked up a couple of stray acorns and flicked them into Haley's pile.

Randall looked over to the mound of tiny acorns tucked just inside the hollow of an oak tree and suddenly beamed.

"I know how we can stop the workers!" he said. "Grab some acorns and follow me."

With his sack bursting with acorns, Randall and Flo headed towards the workers' machinery.

"Good. They must be on their break," Randall said. He crept up to one of the diggers and started to pop the acorns into gaps near the levers and gears.

"This should stop them working," he said.

Flo grinned. "Great. We must have enough acorns here to jam all these diggers. Let me help." She hopped up and joined Randall to fill the equipment with acorns. "Quick!" she whispered. "The humans are coming back."

Randall slipped the last acorns into a digger and they hid behind a tree to watch.

It wasn't long before the humans started their engines. **Whirr, whirr! Crunch! Scrunch!**

There was a grating sound. Randall and Flo looked at each other, pleased. But then there was a yell. The acorns had been spotted. The worker scooped a pile out and threw them on the ground in disgust. He tried again and this time the machinery spluttered into life.

There was a rumble and a ping... ping! "Ouch!" Flo cried as an acorn bounced off her head.

"Ooh... er! I think this acorn trap wasn't such a good idea after all," Randall cried as one hit his furry tail. "Run!"

Acorns whizzed in all directions. They pinged off trees and bounced on the ground. Randall and Flo dashed back through the wood, dodging the flying missiles.

When Randall and Flo had run far enough out of reach, they stopped to rest near the Howling Stones.

But the sight of two humans stopped them in their tracks. The humans had maps and were measuring the Stones.

Flo and Randall crept as near as they dared to hear what the humans were saying.

"The boss wants no more delays," one said.

"Okay." The other nodded. "We'll get these stones cleared tomorrow, that's a promise."

Randall and Flo turned to each other, shocked. "I've failed." Randall uttered a low whine and sank his head onto his paws.

Chapter 6

"You can't give up!" Flo cried and pounded her bunny paws against Randall's soft furry side.

He pushed her gently away. "It's no good, Flo. I've tried everything I can think of and nothing has worked. What sort of guardian am I if I can't save the Howling Stones?"

"There must be a way, there must," Flo said. "What about everyone's homes? Where will we all live?"

"I don't know," Randall shook his head sadly. He rose and gathered his sack.

"Don't give up, Randall. The wood needs you," Flo pleaded. "The creatures need you too," she added quietly, but Randall slunk away. His head drooped and his tail dragged.

That evening, the wolves gathered at the Howling Stones. Randall joined them.

" **AWOOo!** "

they called one by one.

Randall opened his mouth to howl but nothing came out.

"Aw..." He croaked.

The Elders looked at each other.

"What is the matter, young Randall? Have you lost your howl so soon?" Chief Quicksilver gave him a concerned look. One or two of the other wolves grinned.

Randall ignored their smirks. He looked at the ground and shook his head.

"Well, never mind being nervous. You are amongst friends. Try again at our ceremony tomorrow."

But Randall found his voice at last. He burst out, "There won't be a ceremony tomorrow. There won't be any Stones."

"No ceremony? No Stones? Of course there will be, what are you talking about?" Quicksilver stared at him sternly.

"The Stones are going to be knocked down to build homes for humans," Randall blurted out. "I've tried everything I can to stop the workers but it's too late. They're being destroyed tomorrow."

The wolves gasped. There was a murmur of anxious growls.

"Hush!" Quicksilver held up a paw. "Are you certain? If this is true it is very serious indeed, Randall. Why did you not come to us in the first place?"

Randall gulped and looked around at the wolves. The inner circle of Elders loomed over him. He was the smallest one there. He looked down at his paws and sniffed. "I didn't want to worry anyone. I wanted to save the wood all on my own."

He tried not to look at the other wolves and creatures in the wood, who had crept nearer the Stones to hear what was happening. There were so many of them. He wanted to hide, but his legs wouldn't move. They were all looking at him very hard and Quicksilver's nose quivered.

"I'm sorry, I failed," Randall said quietly.

Quicksilver suddenly pushed his nose towards Randall who shrank back. "Hmm..." Quicksilver said. "No one's failed yet. Our fight is not over."

"That's right!" came a squeaky cry. It was Denny the dormouse who had scurried to the centre of the Howling Stones. He whizzed up Randall's leg and squeaked his battle cry again in the little wolf's ear.

There were more squeaks and cheers from Denny's family. The other animals joined in too. Flo, who had sneaked into the circle, squeezed Randall's paw. He looked up to see all the animals. There were big ones, small ones, flying ones, climbing ones, loud ones, even tiny creepy crawly ones. Determination marked their faces.

So many creatures, Randall thought. Suddenly everything seemed possible again. He wasn't alone in his fight to save the Stones... and it was then that he had an idea.

Chapter 7

The next day, the workers arrived with their machinery at the Howling Stones. This time they had brought heavy lifting equipment to shift the Stones. Each stone stood as tall as a man and was made of solid granite.

But surrounding the Stones were seven large wolves with their teeth bared and their hackles up. Inside the stone circle were hundreds of creatures. There were more wolves, rabbits, foxes, owls, hedgehogs, weasels, squirrels and a whole array of birds and crawling insects. Randall stood with Flo by his side at the edge of the Stones. He wasn't going to fail this time.

He heard one of them say, "Shoo! Get away you lot."

But the animals did not move. "Are those wolves?" One of the workers looked frightened. He called out for his boss.

"It's working, it's working," Flo whispered, bouncing up and down.

A stern man in a yellow hardhat holding a map appeared. Randall guessed he must be the boss. He glared at the animals. He shouted and waved his arms.

By now, more workers appeared and people from the village below had come to see what the commotion was about. They looked in awe at the number of animals that confronted them.

Randall sensed the animals' nervousness now they were face to face with more humans and he growled quietly, "Stay firm everyone."

The wolves took their cue from Randall and they began to howl in unison. The other creatures joined in. The workers took a few steps back but remained watching the animals.

Chapter 8

Some time later, the animals watched a sign go up to declare that the Howling Stones, and surrounding woodland, was a protected place.

Flo and Randall smiled and he said, "We've done it. Everyone's homes are safe."

"Hurrah! No humans here and no more noisy diggers," Denny squeaked. "The wood is peaceful once again." He rubbed his pink paws, yawned and promptly fell asleep in Randall's litter sack.

Flo gave Randall a hug. "You did it, you did it," she said. Her eyes shone.

That night when the moon glimmered in the inky black

sky, a special ceremony took place at the Howling Stones. The Wolf Elders took their usual places in a circle and the woodland animals nearby cheered, "Bravo, Randall! You are a true woodland guardian. You saved our homes and the sacred Howling Stones."

But Randall raised a paw. "Thank you friends, but it wasn't just me who saved these magnificent Stones. You should thank yourselves too. Our wood was saved because we all joined together. I think it was a great team effort."

Quicksilver nodded and stroked his grey whiskers. "Not only have you proved you are a true woodland guardian but that you are kind and generous too," he said. "I am growing older and my time as leader is nearly over. Soon a new Elder will be needed for the circle. You are young, Randall, with more to learn, but you have proven to all of us you have the right qualities. Carry on your woodland guardian training and one day you may be ready to join the Elders."

Randall couldn't believe his ears. The chance to be a Wolf Elder was beyond his wildest dreams. He let out a loud, "**AWOOo!**"

There was an echo of approval from the other wolves: "**AWOOo! AWOOo!**"

Discussion Points

1. What role was Randall given in the beginning?

2. Where was Flo stuck?

a) In a pile of logs

b) In a thorny bush

c) High in a tree

3. What was your favourite part of the story?

4. How do Randall and Flo stop the humans' machines?

5. Why do you think the humans decided not to build in the forest?

6. Who was your favourite character and why?

7. There were moments in the story when Randall tried to **protect** his home. Where do you think the story shows this most?

8. What do you think happens after the end of the story?

Book Bands for Guided Reading

The Institute of Education book banding system is a scale of colours that reflects the various levels of reading difficulty. The bands are assigned by taking into account the content, the language style, the layout and phonics. Word, phrase and sentence level work is also taken into consideration.

The Maverick Readers Scheme is a bright, attractive range of books covering the pink to grey bands. All of these books have been book banded for guided reading to the industry standard and edited by a leading educational consultant.

To view the whole Maverick Readers scheme, visit our website at

www.maverickearlyreaders.com

Or scan the QR code to view our scheme instantly!

Maverick Chapter Readers
(From Lime to Grey Band)